THE CANADIAN BRASS
15 FAVORITE HYMNS
EASY ARRANGEMENTS

ARRANGED BY LARRY MOORE

T0040834

Using the Arrangements
A music director/conductor can come up with various approaches to a hymn. For instance: verse 1 – no brass; verse 2 – brass (Standard Version); verse 3 – brass (Variation Verse); verse 4 – brass (Standard Version) with Trumpet Descant. Or, another example might be: verse 1 – brass (Standard Version) with keyboard; verse 2 – brass (Standard Version), no keyboard; verse 3 – brass (Variation Verse). Get creative!

Optional Trumpet Descant
The Conductor's Score also includes the part for a trumpet descant. The descant may be added to any of the Standard Version verses of a hymn. The trumpet part is available in the following Hal Leonard publication: 50485217 *The Canadian Brass: 15 Favorite Hymns–Trumpet Descants*

Visit the official website of The Canadian Brass:
www.canbrass.com

HAL•LEONARD®
CORPORATION
7777 W. BLUEMOUND RD. P.O. BOX 13819 MILWAUKEE, WI 53213

Visit Hal Leonard Online at
www.halleonard.com

ALL CREATURES OF OUR GOD AND KING

LASST UNS ERFREUEN

Francis of Assisi
Trans. W.H. Draper

Geistliche Kirchengesang
Harmonized by Ralph Vaughan Williams

* *rit.* is used only if the Variation Verse is played as the final verse

Return to Standard Version as needed

CANADIAN BRASS
ALL GLORY, LAUD, AND HONOR
ST. THEODULPH

Theodulph of Orleans, ca. 820
Trans. by John Mason Neal, 1851; alt., 1859

Melchior Teschner, 1615

* *rit.* is used only if the Variation Verse is played as the final verse

Return to Standard Version as needed

Horn in F

CANADIAN BRASS

BLESSED ASSURANCE

ASSURANCE

Fanny J. Crosby

Phoebe P. Knapp

* *rit.* is used only if the Variation Verse is played as the final verse

Return to Standard Version as needed

Horn in F

CANADIAN BRASS

CHRIST THE LORD IS RISEN TODAY

EASTER HYMN

Charles Wesley

from *Lyra Davidica*, London, 1708

STANDARD VERSION

Joyously (♩ = 120)

Repeat as needed (opt.)

VARIATION VERSE

(rit.)*

* *rit.* is used only if the Variation Verse is played as the final verse

Return to Standard Version as needed

Horn in F

CANADIAN BRASS

COME, YE THANKFUL PEOPLE, COME

ST. GEORGE'S, WINDSOR

Henry Alford

George J. Elve

* *rit.* is used only if the Variation Verse is played as the final verse

Return to Standard Version as needed

Horn in F

CROWN HIM WITH MANY CROWNS
DIADEMATA

Matthew Bridges, stanzas 1,2,4;
Godfrey Thring, stanza 3

George J. Elvey

* *rit.* is used only if the Variation Verse is played as the final verse

Return to Standard Version as needed

Horn in F

CANADIAN BRASS

FAIREST LORD JESUS
(Beautiful Savior)
CRUSADERS' HYMN

Anonymous German Hymn, *Munster Gesangbuch*, 1677;
translated, Source unknown, stanzas 1-3; Joseph A. Seiss, Stanza 4

Schlesische Volkslieder, 1842
arranged by Richard S. Willi

STANDARD VERSION
Reverently (♩ = 84)

Repeat as needed (opt.)   Amen

VARIATION VERSE

Return to Standard Version as neede

Horn in F

CANADIAN BRASS

FOR THE BEAUTY OF THE EARTH

DIX

Folliott S. Pierpoint, altered

Conrad Cocher;
arranged by William H. Monk

* *rit.* is used only if the Variation Verse is played as the final verse

Return to Standard Version as needed

Horn in F

CANADIAN BRASS

GOD OF OUR FATHERS

NATIONAL HYMN

Daniel C. Roberts

George W. Warren

* *rit.* is used only if the Variation Verse is played as the final verse

Return to Standard Version as needed

Horn in F

GUIDE ME, O THOU GREAT JEHOVAH
(God of Grace and God of Glory)

CWM RHONDDA

William Williams;
translated by Peter Williams

John Hughes

* *rit.* is used only if the Variation Verse is played as the final verse

Return to Standard Version as needed

Horn in F

CANADIAN BRASS

HOLY, HOLY, HOLY!

NICEA

Reginald Heber

John B. Dykes

* *rit.* is used only if the Variation Verse is played as the final verse

Return to Standard Version as needed

Horn in F

CANADIAN BRASS

JOYFUL, JOYFUL, WE ADORE THEE

HYMN TO JOY

Henry van Dyke

Ludwig van Beethoven

* *rit.* is used only if the Variation Verse is played as the final verse

Return to Standard Version as needed

Horn in F

CANADIAN BRASS

LEAD ON, O KING ETERNAL

LANCASHIRE

Ernest W. Shurtleff

Henry T. Smart

* *rit.* is used only if the Variation Verse is played as the final verse

Return to Standard Version as needed

Horn in F

CANADIAN BRASS

A MIGHTY FORTRESS IS OUR GOD

EIN FESTE BURG

Martin Luther
Trans. by F.H. Hedge, based on Psalm 46

Martin Luther

* *rit.* is used only if the Variation Verse is played as the final verse

Return to Standard Version as needed

Horn in F

CANADIAN BRASS

O GOD, OUR HELP IN AGES PAST

ST. ANNE

Isaac Watts;
based on Psalm 90

attr. William Croft

STANDARD VERSION
Joyously (♩ = 100)

mf

Repeat as needed (opt.)   Amen   VARIATION VERSE

(rit.)*

* *rit.* is used only if the Variation Verse is played as the final verse

Return to Standard Version as needed